W9-ANZ-644

TIGER RESCUE

TIGER RESCUE

Changing the Future for Endangered Wildlife

DAN BORTOLOTTI

FIREFLY BOOKS

A FIREFLY BOOK

Published by Firefly Books Ltd. 2003

First printing

PUBLISHER CATALOGING-IN-PUBLICATION DATA (U.S.)
(Library of Congress Standards)
Bortolotti, Dan.
Tiger rescue : changing the future for endangered wildlife / Dan Bortolotti. –1st ed.
[64] p. : col. photos. ;   cm.   (Firefly animal rescue)
Includes bibliographical references and index.
Summary: An exploration of tigers, their various habitats, the threat of extinction,
and the conservationists who are working with them.
ISBN 1-55297-599-1
ISBN 1-55297-558-4 (pbk.)
1. Tigers—Juvenile literature. 2. Endangered species—Juvenile literature. I. Title. II. Series.
578.68 21   QL737.C23.B67 2003

NATIONAL LIBRARY OF CANADA CATALOGUING IN PUBLICATION DATA
Bortolotti, Dan
Tiger rescue : changing the future for endangered wildlife / Dan Bortolotti.
(Firefly animal resue)
Includes index.
ISBN 1-55297-599-1 (bound).—ISBN 1-55297-558-4 (pbk.)
1. Tigers. I. Title. II. Series.
QL737.C23B67 2003   599.756   C2003-902824-0

Published in the United States in 2003 by
Firefly Books (U.S.) Inc.
P.O. Box 1338, Ellicott Station
Buffalo, New York 14205

Published in Canada in 2003 by
Firefly Books Ltd.
3680 Victoria Park Avenue
Toronto, Ontario, M2H 3K1

Design: Ingrid Paulson
Maps: Roberta Cooke

Printed in Canada by Friesens, Altona, Manitoba

*The Publisher acknowledges the financial support of the Government of Canada through the
Book Publishing Industry Development Program for its publishing activities.*

TABLE OF CONTENTS

KING OF THE CATS

It is both beautiful and terrible. It stalks its prey silently, but defends its kills with a fearsome roar. Its face looks as harmless as a house cat's on cereal boxes and plush toys, while in the wild it makes half-ton mammals flee for their lives. Outside of circuses and zoos, it is as foreign to the Western hemisphere as the kangaroo. And yet the magnificent tiger has found its way into our hearts.

Panthera tigris is the largest of the 38 cat species—more massive even than the lion, the so-called king of the beasts. Despite a popular misconception, it did not evolve from the extinct Smilodon, or "saber-toothed tiger." The modern tiger originated in eastern Asia about two million years ago, and from there spread to central Asia, the Russian Far East, India and the islands of Indonesia.

Today tigers inhabit many of these same areas, but in dramatically fewer numbers. There may have been more than 100,000 tigers in the wild in 1900. A century later, that number is probably between 5,000 and 7,000. Hunting, habitat destruction and dwindling prey have pushed the wild tiger to the brink of extinction. As recently as the 1990s, many people believed it would not survive into the new millennium.

But survive it has, thanks to the work of scientists, park rangers, government officials and conservationists around the world—in India, China, Indonesia and Russia, and in many countries where wild tigers have never roamed.

Of course, this is an animal that can kill prey four times its size. No one really expected it would go down without a fight.

WHERE DO TIGERS LIVE?

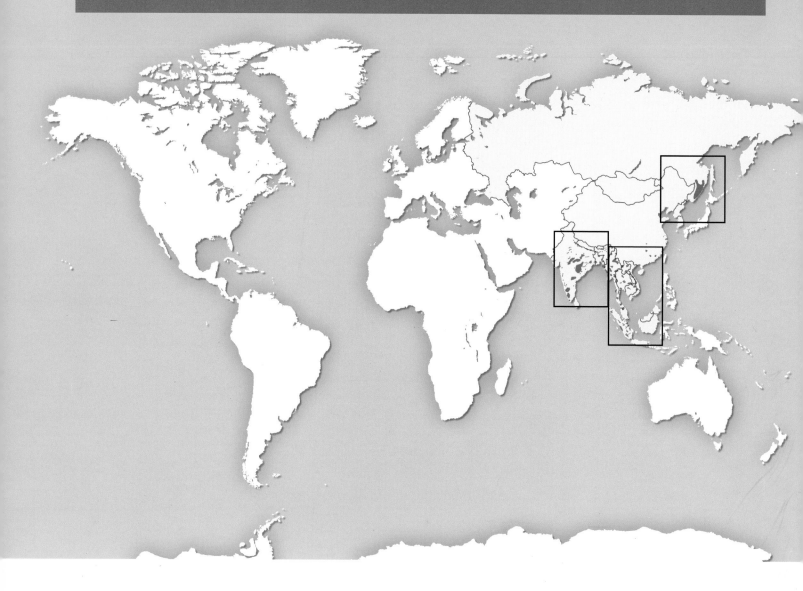

Five subspecies of tiger currently live in 14 Asian countries.

Amur or **Siberian tigers** (*Panthera tigris altaica*) are the largest and most familiar. There are only 400 or so in the wild, mostly in the Russian Far East.

Indian or **Bengal tigers** (*Panthera tigris tigris*) are the most common in the wild, with about 4,000 living throughout the Indian subcontinent.

Indochinese tigers (*Panthera tigris corbetti*) live in Cambodia, Malaysia, Thailand, Vietnam and other parts of Southeast Asia. Scientists estimate there are around 1,500 in the wild.

South China or **Chinese tigers** (*Panthera tigris amoyensis*) are extremely rare — perhaps fewer than 30 exist in the wild, all in southern and central China.

Sumatran tigers (*Panthera tigris sumatrae*) are all on the island of Sumatra in Indonesia. The most recent estimate puts the population at about 400 in the wild.

THE STORY SO FAR

Until the 1960s, few people thought that wild tigers might one day disappear. Although their numbers had plummeted, the idea of conservation was still almost unheard of. Meanwhile, at least one subspecies, the Bali tiger, had quietly slipped into oblivion.

When the world finally awoke to the plight of the tiger, it went into damage-control mode. In the early 1970s, particularly in India, governments and conservation groups worked quickly to try to protect its habitat and to stop the trade in its parts. It all came too late for the Caspian and Javan tigers which were both extinct by the end of the decade. But things were looking up in India, at least.

By the mid-1980s the momentum had shifted again: poachers were killing hundreds of animals, and it looked like the wild tiger might not make it to the year 2000.

∧ A Russian official displays a tiger skin confiscated under CITES in March 2002.

1967 U.S. zoologist and conservationist George Schaller publishes *The Deer and the Tiger*, the first scientific study of tigers in the wild.

1969 The Indian tiger, the most common subspecies, is declared officially endangered by the International Union for Conservation of Nature and Natural Resources. The tiger population in India is estimated at 2,500.

1972 India becomes the first nation to commit to protecting tiger habitat. Bangladesh and Nepal soon announce similar programs.

1973 Project Tiger is born in India, and Corbett National Park becomes its first reserve. Eight more follow within a year.

1975 Eighteen countries agree to the Convention on International Trade in Endangered Species of Wild Fauna and Flora (CITES). It calls for a total ban on the trade in tiger products. Nepal is the first tiger-range state to sign; India follows in 1976.

1980 After a dramatic rise in the wild population, the director of Project Tiger declares his country's efforts a success: "There is now no danger of extinction of the tiger in India." The celebration is premature.

1981 The Chinese government signs CITES but continues to be criticized for turning a blind eye to the tiger trade.

1986 Several tigers are poached in the Dudhwa reserve in India. Conservationists suspect that the black-market supply of tiger bone must be running low for the first time in decades.

1989 The population of Amur tigers in the Soviet Union is estimated at 400. By 1993, poachers will reduce the number to about 150.

1993 Several high-profile incidents of poaching—and huge seizures of tiger bone—sound alarm bells. An international report suggests that poaching alone could soon wipe out the wild tiger.

1994 *Time* magazine carries the face of a tiger with an ominous coverline: "Doomed." "Once considered a conservation success story," the issue says, "they are again sliding toward extinction."

1995 Exxon Corporation, which has used the tiger on its logo for almost a century, creates the Save the Tiger Fund and commits $5 million (U.S.) over five years.

1997 WWF launches its Tiger Conservation Programme to give additional support to Project Tiger. Myanmar (formerly Burma) and Cambodia join CITES.

2003 The European Association of Zoos and Aquaria completes its Tiger Campaign, raising more than €250,000 (about $275,000 U.S.) to support conservation projects in India, Russia and Indonesia.

HOME IS WHERE THE HUNT IS

Tigers are remarkably adaptable and live in a variety of habitats, from tropical rainforests to mountainous woodlands, from dry grasslands to mangrove swamps. While most live in warm climates, they can tolerate a wide range of temperatures: the Amur tiger can survive temperatures well below −40°F/C.

Tiger habitat must have three things: water, dense vegetation and a healthy supply of large prey.

Unlike other cats, tigers enjoy the water—they often cool themselves and escape insects in rivers and ponds, and they are strong swimmers. While their lion cousins hunt in open areas and share their prey with others, tigers hunt alone and expect to dine alone. So they need the cover of forests to conceal themselves and their kills. Most importantly, tigers need a variety of animals, especially hoofed mammals to feed upon.

Despite the animal's flexibility, the amount of its suitable habitat is shrinking fast. Tigers are skilled hunters, but they can't compete with humans who use guns to kill the same prey. Logging companies and local villagers cut down forests for lumber and to make way for farming, forcing the tiger into smaller and smaller areas.

As human populations increase throughout the tiger's range, many believe that tigers will never again roam the wilderness in great numbers. The animal's only hope for long-term survival may be in wildlife reserves, which are protected from the chainsaw and where large prey are allowed to run free.

NO TRESPASSING

Tigers are solitary animals. Even when several inhabit a common area, they usually do their best to avoid one another.

All tigers stake out a particular area as their territory. The size depends almost entirely on the amount of available prey, and can vary enormously. In parts of Nepal that are teeming with potential tiger prey, territories can be as small as 6 square miles (10 km²) for females and perhaps twice that for males. In Russia, where meals are much harder to come by, a male's territory can exceed 600 square miles (1,000 km²).

To mark their territory, tigers leave scent clues — they deposit urine, feces and other secretions to tell others to stay away. They may also rear up on their hind legs and scratch trees with their forepaws. Other tigers happening upon these markings can tell how long ago they were left, and whether they were made by a familiar tiger or a stranger. Females in heat also use scent markings to let males know they're nearby.

TIGER TRACKING

Rescuing the wild tiger from possible extinction takes close study; conservationists first need to understand the animal's habits and behavior.

One of the first things conservation groups must do is get an accurate head count of the tigers in a particular area. Unfortunately, the tiger is elusive and the territories it occupies can be vast and remote. So scientists have developed techniques to help them get accurate numbers.

Trained eyes can recognize a tiger's territorial markings—scratch marks, feces, urine sprays—and the remains of kills. Paw prints, or pugmarks, are another distinctive calling card. Because tiger forepaws suffer injuries fighting over territory and with large prey, some have obvious markings that can be recorded and compared. Trackers identify individual tigers this way, although some scientists believe the method is not at all reliable.

∧ A researcher raises an antenna to detect signals from tigers outfitted with radio collars.

More recently, scientists have used remote cameras that automatically photograph tigers when they walk past. These cameras are unobtrusive and can provide clear pictures of the animals' stripe patterns. Just as every person has a different set of fingerprints, every tiger has a unique pattern of stripes.

When they want to follow the movements of a tiger over a long period, scientists may use radio telemetry. First, they have to capture the tiger by setting specially designed snares that hold the animal's leg without harming it. From a safe distance, they shoot the tiger with a tranquilizing dart, then fit the unconscious animal with a radio collar that can reveal its location at any time.

< Scientists fit a tranquilized tiger with a radio collar, which allows them to track its movements and study its behavior.

As recently as the 1990s, no one knew for certain whether any South China tigers remained in the wild. There were many reports of scratch marks, remains of kills, even roars — but nothing conclusive. Then there was a sighting in 1999, and the following year zoologists found pugmarks and scats (feces) that were unmistakable. The South China tiger was still around.

∧ A tiger statue marks the entrance to the Meihuashan South China Tiger Breeding and Rehabilitation Centre.

But the prognosis is bleak: the wild population is probably less than 30, and many conservation organizations think the subspecies is beyond hope. They argue that resources would be better spent on populations that are more likely to recover.

Li Quan isn't having any of that. Quan was born and raised in Beijing, China, studied business in the United States and established a career in Italy's luxury-fashion industry. Then in October 2000, while living in London, England, she founded Save China's Tigers. Quan is determined not to let *Panthera tigris amoyensis* go the way of last year's clothing designs.

"For thousands of years, the tiger has played a big part in Chinese traditions and beliefs, becoming a symbol of power and strength, a subject of awe and fear," Quan says. "China is determined to save the tiger. Its success or failure is a matter of honor or shame to the Chinese people."

The Chinese government, with the support of Save China's Tigers and a team of foreign experts, hopes to expand and rehabilitate the nature reserves where tigers are known to live. Ideally, these forests would be protected from logging and poaching, and patrols would make sure the laws were respected.

Li Quan (*right*) and Liao Xiansheng check a map during an expedition to the Hupingshan Nature Reserve.

The largest of these protected areas would be Luoxiao Mountain, which covers more than 3,600 square miles (6,000 km²) and spans five nature reserves in three provinces. The plan is to connect the reserves — allowing the tiny tiger populations a chance to mingle — by converting 27,500 acres (11,000 ha) of farmland back into forest, and by introducing prey. The Chinese government also believes that wild tigers would bring ecotourism dollars to the area, which in turn would encourage local people to support the conservation efforts.

In 2002, Save China's Tigers and the country's State Forestry Administration drew up a plan to reintroduce tigers to the wild. Selected cubs in Chinese zoos will travel to South Africa—a country that has no native tigers, but plenty of experience in rehabilitating cat populations. There the tigers will be trained to hunt in a protected area of more than 185 square miles (300 km²). If all goes as planned, some of their descendents will be brought back to China five to six years later to be turned loose in the reclaimed forests.

"We unfortunately can't tell just how many Chinese tigers are left," Li Quan admits. "But we're paving the way for their survival."

DONE LIKE DINNER

All cats are meat eaters, but tigers take it a step further. They are what scientists call hypercarnivores, meaning that their diet consists almost solely of the flesh of other vertebrates.

Of course, predators can't always afford to be selective. Like other hunters, tigers are forced to prey on whatever they can find. The tiger's bread and butter is the meat of ungulates (hoofed mammals), especially wild deer, cattle and boar. Depending on the tiger's range, prey includes elk and antelope; sambar, chital and other deer; and the massive gaur and banteng (two types of wild oxen). When the pickings are truly slim, tigers will munch grass, berries, eggs or fruits, and have been known to eat frogs, fish, snakes, lizards and even insects. They will also occasionally scavenge the kills of other animals.

The tiger's rule of thumb when selecting prey is simple: the bigger the better. They typically try to kill the largest mammal available to them, even ignoring smaller animals that might be easier to catch. After all, the energy spent in chasing a dozen hares may not be worth what they'd gain from eating them. On the other hand, while more difficult to take down, a big animal can provide enough food for several days.

After a successful hunt, tigers will eat an average of 33 to 40 pounds (15 to 18 kg) in a single night, usually in hour-long stretches with rests in between. Very large, hungry males—and these can weigh up to 660 pounds (300 kg)—may devour 75 pounds (34 kg) of meat in a day. After a meal like that a tiger will, not surprisingly, go a few days before eating again.

The tiger's rule of thumb is simple: the bigger the prey, the better.

< After making a kill, tigers use their enormously strong jaws to drag the prey into a concealed area. They will return to feed on a large carcass for several days.

PREDATOR-IN-CHIEF

The tiger is a crown predator, which means that it's at the very top of the food chain, where it looks down on a large selection of menu items.

It's a vulnerable position, since a change in any one species' population will ultimately affect the health of those above it on the chain. Call it the trickle-up effect. For this reason the tiger is called an "indicator species" —it's used to measure the health of its entire ecosystem. If it's thriving, chances are almost everything else is too.

Despite its prowess as a hunter, the tiger may wander 20 miles (32 km) in a single night without snaring a meal. And most of the animals it pursues can outrun their enemy, unless they're surprised. As a result, tigers are successful in making a kill only once in 10 or 20 attempts— about every five to eight days.

As the amount of prey increases in any area, so does the number of tigers. This predator goes through a lot of meat: a well-fed adult kills about 6,600 pounds (3,000 kg) of prey each year, or perhaps 40 to 50 animals. Females with cubs in tow need even more.

Unfortunately, the tiger has to share this prey with other hunters, including people. Conservationists now realize that the overhunting of potential tiger prey by humans is a major reason why tiger populations are shrinking, even in habitats that are otherwise healthy.

While the tiger stands at the top of the food chain and is an excellent hunter,   >
it is successful in making a kill only once every five to eight days.

ANATOMY OF A HUNT

A tiger taking down its prey is one of nature's great spectacles. Like a thunderstorm, it begins with an eerie calm as the predator stalks its victim, and then explodes into violence as the tiger attacks.

When a tiger spots a potential victim, the dance begins: The tiger remains hidden in the grass while silently creeping within 30 to 60 feet (10 to 20 m) of its quarry. Tigers do not roar as they attack—the sound would scare off the prey. However, some experts believe, though it hasn't been scientifically proven, that tigers can emit a low-frequency growl, inaudible to humans, that can stun an animal and prevent it from fleeing.

Once it is within range, the tiger explodes out of its hiding place. It extends its claws, transforming its paws from tools of stealth into deadly weapons. The tiger then pounces from behind and holds on while attempting to sink its huge canines into the animal's neck.

It extends its claws, transforming its paws from tools of stealth into deadly weapons.

Next comes the takedown. Since the tiger often hunts animals heavier than itself, it has learned to wait for the prey to move first, and then use the animal's own momentum to bring it down. This is similar to the way a martial artist takes down an opponent.

If the prey is small, the tiger tries to crush its vertebrae and sever the spinal cord, killing it almost instantly. When going after larger mammals, it tries to puncture the trachea, holding on to the throat until the animal suffocates, which can take several minutes.

When the prey is dead, the tiger drags its kill into an area with some cover to discourage other animals from scavenging its prize. It will often return to a large kill for several days.

ndia is home to more than half of the world's wild tigers, and in the early 1970s it became the first country to get serious about saving them. Project Tiger, now more than 30 years old, is the most ambitious and controversial plan ever undertaken to save the animal.

∧ The body of a tiger—probably poisoned in retaliation for killing livestock—arrives to be autopsied by Project Tiger.

"Project Tiger, along with an Indian law called the Wildlife Protection Act, has been the most successful tiger conservation initiative in any tiger-range country," says zoologist Ullas Karanth, director of the Wildlife Conservation Society's India Program. "Given that India has a billion people and umpteen problems, this is not to be scoffed at."

In 1969, when the Indian tiger was finally recognized as an endangered species, World Wildlife Fund (WWF) raised $1 million (U.S.) to get things rolling. With the personal blessing of Indira Gandhi, India's then-prime minister, the country launched Project Tiger in 1973, creating nine protected areas. It was an enormous job: entire villages were moved. Farmers faced fines if they allowed their animals to graze in the reserves. Scientists set up cameras and radio-tracking equipment, while patrols and bureaucrats made sure everything went smoothly. Today there are 25 Project Tiger reserves.

All the work began to pay off. By 1979, the tiger population in India was said to have reached 3,300 —up by more than a thousand from a decade earlier. Many people felt that the tiger was out of danger. They were wrong.

By the early 1990s, it was clear that Project Tiger was losing ground. The tiger trade was on the rise, and India's comparatively healthy tiger populations were the easiest target for poachers, who managed to elude patrols. India's population grew by 300 million people (and 100 million livestock) between 1973 and 1993, straining the boundaries of the reserves. And wildlife conservation became much less of a priority for governments and the public.

Ullas Karanth (*right*) and a colleague examine a tranquilized cat. Karanth has criticized what he feels are inaccurate tiger population counts in India.

The Hindu religion places a high value on all life, and its followers, who make up about 80 percent of India's people, are generally willing to protect endangered species. But even the most generous people are unlikely to show enthusiasm for a program that threatens their livelihood. In the mid-1990s it was common for villagers to kill tigers in retaliation for attacks on their livestock. In one high-profile case in Dudhwa Tiger Reserve in 1998, farmers poisoned a female and her three cubs.

To further confuse matters, the tiger population figures that officials had bandied about were probably wildly inaccurate. "All these numbers are based on invalid methods and bad science. They have no relation to real population trends," says Ullas Karanth. "In some cases they were overestimated, but in many others they were probably underestimated, too." Bureaucrats, under enormous pressure to show results, were accused of intentionally exaggerating the numbers.

The good news is that, since about 1997, Project Tiger is heading back on track, thanks to some dynamic leadership and the help of several conservation organizations. Karanth believes that with proper management of the reserves, tiger populations can again recover. "There is still about 300,000 square kilometers of potential tiger habitat remaining in India, of which only about 10 percent is effectively protected now. Our recent scientific studies show that tigers can attain very high densities of 10 to 15 animals per 100 square kilometers in Indian reserves. So there is still room for a lot more tigers."

Conservationists and governments also realize how important it is to bring local people on board and help them benefit from the tiger's recovery. To prevent incidents like the Dudwha killing, some Indian states offer a kind of "tiger insurance" that pays farmers for livestock killed by tigers. But many experts feel these compensation plans simply don't work, and they're looking for other solutions. Judy Mills, a former WWF tiger specialist, thinks it makes more sense to pay people before trouble arises. "For example, a village with a tiger in its forest might receive a monthly or annual payment for tolerating the tiger and perhaps even keeping track of its movements," she explains. "The rate might go up if the tiger has cubs. The idea is to reward locals for positive actions."

In ritual mass hunts, some tribal communities set fire to forests and kill potential tiger prey.

In other parts of India, the cultural challenges are greater. In Simlipal Tiger Reserve, people organize an annual mass hunt called *akhand shikar*, in which forests are set ablaze and hundreds of animals are killed. This ritual doesn't usually include hunting tigers, but the toll it takes on their prey is enormous. WWF is working with the tribal leaders to encourage other, less damaging rituals, such as dance and archery competitions. As Mills says, "This is the only way tiger conservation will be sustainable."

Growing up in Bangalore, India, Praveen Bhargav enjoyed catching snakes and photographing wildlife. By age 18, he was organizing nature camps for schoolchildren and volunteering as a national park guide. Now he's blazing a new trail in tiger conservation.

Bhargav is the managing trustee of Wildlife First, an organization working to ensure that sanctuaries and reserves are truly protected.

One of the activities he's involved in is a resettlement project in Nagarahole National Park, in southern India. About 6,000 Jenu Kurubas (members of a tribal community) live within the boundaries of Nagarahole and work on coffee plantations outside the park. Wildlife First—with the help of several other partners—is encouraging these people to resettle in another area. It's difficult and controversial work, but it may be the only sustainable way to protect tigers and other endangered mammals.

Bhargav stresses that the people are not being forced from their homes. "The process has been truly voluntary," he says of the more than 250 families who have agreed to move. In return the Indian government has given them each 5 acres of farmland, housing, electricity, health care, access to drinking water, training and other amenities they could not have hoped for before. "Our win-win strategy is to deliver social justice to the people and, at the same time, reduce habitat fragmentation and permanently resolve human-tiger conflict."

Villagers who have recently moved from Nagarahole pose in front of their new community hall. So far, at least 250 families have voluntarily resettled.

A businessman who has studied marketing and advertising, Bhargav has delivered his message in innovative ways. In 1997, he created a TV campaign in which Indian cricket stars spoke out about tiger conservation; the spots were aired on major international networks.

> Not all of his work is quite so glamorous, however. Over the years, Bhargav has given workshops; challenged illegal mining, logging and forest encroachment in the courts; lobbied the government and trained anti-poaching guards. For his efforts, India made him an Honorary Wildlife Warden in 1997, and in 2001 he received the Esso Award for Tiger Conservation.

Bhargav knows he has many years of work ahead. About 300 more families are waiting to be moved out of Nagarahole, and he's completing a bigger resettlement project in the nearby Bhadra Tiger Reserve. He's confident the strategy is the right one, though he doesn't expect to see results overnight. "Nagarahole and Bhadra require long-term conservation effort — and Wildlife First is committed to it."

THE TIGER'S ONLY PREDATOR

T he tiger's only serious threat in the animal kingdom is from *Homo sapiens*. For hundreds of years, humans have killed them—for sport, for their body parts, and to defend themselves and their livestock.

As human populations in Asia swelled during the 20th century, tigers and people clashed even more often. Some governments rewarded people for shooting tigers: this went on in China until 1977. In India—a British colony until 1947—the English made an entertainment of hunting wild cats. Even Prince Philip, husband of Queen Elizabeth II and now an active conservationist, shot a tiger during a royal visit in 1961.

India passed a law against hunting tigers in 1970, and today the practice is banned in all 14 countries where wild populations still live. Unfortunately, the killing hasn't stopped. Villagers continue to shoot tigers that are a genuine threat to people or farm animals. Much more worrisome to conservationists are poachers—outlaw hunters who kill tigers to sell their skins, bones and other body parts on the black market.

Even if tigers are no longer slaughtered in huge numbers, illegal hunting can still spell extinction. The death of a female tiger means doom for her offspring if they cannot yet live on their own, and one male's death can cause territorial scraps and upset breeding patterns for years. Unlike deer and oxen, whose numbers are accustomed to being thinned by carnivores, the tiger has no natural predator. So even a few poachers' bullets can tip nature's balance and threaten the whole population.

∧ Poachers sometimes place steel traps alongside paths frequented by tigers. Poison is another favorite: it can be added to the carcass of a domestic animal that is then left for a tiger to scavenge.

31

THE TIGER TRADE

Back when shooting them was legal, bagging a tiger was considered a great accomplishment, and their skins made magnificent trophies. Today tigers are poached for different reasons.

∧ Officials examine a seizure of tiger and leopard skins in Calcutta, India.

Tiger bone is an ingredient in traditional Chinese medicine, most commonly as a treatment for rheumatoid arthritis, or pain and swelling in the joints. Although it has been used for centuries, it wasn't until the late 1980s that tigers were being poached specifically for this reason. Conservationists believe that so many tigers were killed as "pests" in China during the 1950s and 1960s that the stockpile of tiger bones was huge. When that supply ran low, poachers picked up the slack. The situation was so dire by the early 1990s that many people felt the bone trade would spell doom for the tiger.

The tiger's fate is not just bred in the bone. In many Asian countries, all manner of tiger parts—meat, fat, even urine and feces—are used to make folk remedies. Tiger teeth are ground into a powder and used to relieve fever, and gall bladder is a treatment for diabetes. Eyes may be eaten to relieve epilepsy or malaria. Tiger penis is made into a soup and served as a sexual tonic. Teeth and claws are also used to make amulets and jewelry. And while they're not as popular as they once were—probably because they're easy for authorities to identify—skins are still bought and sold.

People who consume tiger-based medicines believe that the power and strength of the tiger will be transferred to them. It's a sad irony that the use these products threatens to extinguish the very source of that power and strength.

People who have never used traditional Chinese medicine (TCM) often dismiss it as superstition. Can tiger bone really do what TCM practitioners claim?

"TCM isn't just something that's been practiced for thousands of years, it's also a science," says Cao Dan of World Wildlife Fund. "They have labs, they have clinical trials. But for tiger bone, there's never been any specific study that's proven it's effective." Even Western scientists agree that calcium — the main ingredient in all animal bone — is an anti-inflammatory, which would make it an appropriate treatment for arthritis. But there's no proof that the calcium has to come from tiger bone.

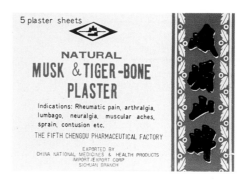

∧ Tiger bone is used in traditional Chinese medicine as a treatment for arthritis and other kinds of joint pain.

In fact, some Asian medicines that claim to be tiger bone may actually contain the bones of other animals. Processing bones to manufacture medicine destroys any DNA, so there's no way to test where they came from.

"When I mention tiger bones, most TCM practitioners immediately say they don't use them anymore," says Cao. "For one thing, it's illegal. Others say they can't find any more." While tiger-bone fakes are designed to deceive, some practitioners are now openly promoting substitutes, such as cattle or pig bones.

When Cao Dan discusses traditional Chinese medicine, she speaks the same language as her audience. "I was raised in China by my grandmother," says Cao, who now lives in Washington, D.C., and heads World Wildlife Fund's TCM program. "When I was sick she used traditional methods to treat me."

Cao even remembers her grandmother preparing a cast made from tiger bone to treat her injured knee. "It was widely available in China at that time. It was only after I came to the States that I realized those things were from endangered species."

Today Cao educates TCM practitioners about the threats to tigers and other endangered animals and plants. She points out that wildlife isn't the only thing that will disappear if the harvest continues. "I say to them, 'If you want to continue this practice and this heritage, it's not going to last long.' They can't ignore the fact that these species are more and more endangered. They need to prescribe these things every day. They suffer from the loss as well. The fundamental philosophy of TCM is harmony and balance between nature and humans. Now there is no balance, because humans take too much from nature."

Her understanding of TCM and Chinese culture gives Cao credibility with Asian practitioners, many of whom are skeptical of Western medical practices. She knows she can't simply march into their office and demand they change their ways. Tiger bones, for example, are virtually identical to those of other animals, but Cao doesn't waste time arguing about chemistry. "The tiger has been treated as a symbol of wisdom and power for centuries. We can't just go to them and say, 'This doesn't work.' They would say, 'Well, it worked on my grandfather.'"

Cao and WWF promote their message in professional journals, encourage TCM manufacturers to use widely available herbs, and work closely with the American College of Traditional Chinese Medicine. She attends TCM conventions and hands out brochures, since many people are still unaware of the laws and regulations.

"We've done so much educational outreach in the last 10 years, and the community understands the issue much better." For example, a 1997 survey found that only 60 percent of TCM practitioners knew that tigers were endangered. By 2001 that figure had increased to 90 percent.

Cao feels that eventually the TCM practitioners will restore that balance and harmony. "It's not an overnight thing, but they realize there's no other way if they want to continue their practice."

"The tiger has been treated as a symbol of wisdom and power for centuries. We can't just go to them and say, 'This doesn't work.'"

Even wild animals can be the victims of politics. In 1991, the powerful Soviet Union dissolved into a group of smaller, independent states. In the turmoil that followed there was a wave of lawlessness, including environmental crimes such as dumping, illegal timber cutting and poaching. One of the hardest-hit animals was the Amur tiger, which was being killed at a rate of 50 to 70 individuals annually. The population was reduced to around 150 tigers. Faced with this grim decline, several conservation groups met with Russian officials in December 1993 and hatched a plan that became Inspection Tiger.

The following year, 15 rangers made their way into a huge forested region in the Russian Far East, inspecting vehicles, seizing weapons and checking up on hunters. "In some areas, the presence of rangers alone is enough to scare poachers away," says Tatiana Dmitrenko, who worked on the project with Phoenix Fund, a conservation group in Vladivostok. "In other areas, rangers take the time to talk to the people they encounter during patrols and explain what they can do to help their home, rather than destroy it."

Sometimes, though, the exchanges are not so friendly. In May 1995, for example, one ranger was attacked and severely beaten by men connected to a ring of smugglers. In general, though, criminals in the tiger trade are much more likely to be prosecuted today than they were in the early 1990s.

Despite the hurdles, Inspection Tiger has been a roaring success. Within eight months of its launch, the killing had already slowed down. The patrol teams — which have grown to include 32 rangers — have reduced poaching by 60 to 80 percent, and the Amur tiger population has climbed above 400 animals again.

The number of Amur tigers dropped drastically after 1991, but Russian patrols have since been very effective in reducing poaching and helping the population recover. Still only about 400 wild tigers remain in Russia.

Dmitrenko says a chief reason is the steady funding from international organizations. But there's more than money at work here. "First of all, it's the people: their motivation, the energy they invested from the start, and their genuine desire to make a difference. The rangers represent a wide range of backgrounds — police, military, security, biology — and it's amazing when you see all these people uniting to put an end to poaching and wildlife trade."

THE GREAT DIVIDE

Stories of poaching and images of seized tiger products grab news headlines and win the attention of people around the world. But there's a far greater threat that gets less attention: the destruction of the tiger's habitat.

∧ Tigers live in some of the most densely populated countries on earth. In Asia, thousands of square miles of forest are cleared every year for agriculture and livestock.

An Indonesian myth holds that man and the tiger made an ancient pact to stay out of each other's way: the tiger would rule the forests and man would rule the farms and villages. Humans haven't kept up their end of the bargain. Tigers live in some of the most densely populated countries on earth. India, the only nation with more than a few hundred tigers, has a population of more than a billion people. Vietnam, home to about 500 tigers, has doubled its population since 1970 and is now one of the most crowded countries in the world. In all, the 14 tiger-range states are home to about half of our planet's population.

All of these people need land for agriculture and livestock, so thousands of square miles of forest are cleared in Asia every year. These people also need meat, and they often hunt the same animals that tigers do. As the amount of suitable land and prey shrinks, tiger populations shrink with them. Those left are broken into islands of very few animals, making the gene pool dangerously shallow. These small groups are also especially vulnerable to natural disasters such as forest fires, monsoon floods and disease.

Spotted deer graze in a tiger reserve that is also coveted agricultural land. Competition between humans and tigers is ongoing, and the big cats usually lose the battles.

While most range states have designated parks and reserves that offer some protection, tigers and humans still clash at the borders. Small reserves of a few hundred square miles, home to a few dozen tigers or less, can be surrounded by villages of hundreds of thousands of people. In the long run, tigers usually lose in these clashes.

L ike all the subspecies, the Indochinese tiger is threatened by poaching and the uncontrolled destruction of forests. But to make its situation uniquely challenging, efforts to conserve this tiger can be mired by war, uncooperative governments, and the remoteness of the terrain, which makes counting and studying animals difficult.

Efforts to save this tiger can mired by war, uncooperative governments and remote terrain.

Panthera tigris corbetti roams the forests of Thailand, Cambodia, Laos, Vietnam, Myanmar and Malaysia. These countries are crowded, facing widespread poverty, and they often place a low priority on stopping the tiger trade.

"Tiger conservationists in southeast Asia need to play many roles: politician, socioeconomist, scientist, diplomat and forester," says Mohamad Azlan, a former science officer with WWF Malaysia.

Hunting Indochinese tigers is banned everywhere. Still, these animals do not benefit from wildlife reserves to the extent that tigers in India do. "Most of the tigers in Peninsular Malaysia may occur outside protected areas," Azlan explains. "Our study site can be converted for agriculture or logging by the state government if it wishes to do so."

Because tigers are so difficult to track in the remote forests of southeast Asia, camera traps are set up to automatically photograph the animals as they walk by.

Launched in 1998, WWF's project in Malaysia is designed to prevent clashes with people. For example, farmers in the area often allow their livestock to roam freely, which invites tiger trouble. "Domesticated animals are much easier to hunt, as they have reduced escape capabilities," Azlan says. "When artificial prey is abundant, tiger populations around human settlement may increase. This is where the conflict occurs." Azlan and WWF advise farmers to keep their animals locked safely in paddocks between 6 p.m. and 9 a.m., since this is the tiger's prime hunting time.

In order to stop tigers from preying on livestock, farmers are encouraged to keep their animals in paddocks during the night.

Of course, money is always a problem. "The farmers are very poor. Sometimes they make less than 10 ringgit a month—that's about $2 or $3 U.S. So I am trying to find funds or materials for the farmers to build reasonable paddocks for their cattle. It is very difficult to raise such resources in a developing country like Malaysia." Fortunately, wwf's Tiger Emergency Fund recently supplied the project with a grant, which provided paddocks for several farmers.

Experience has taught Azlan that if tigers and people are going to live together, it's not the tigers that have to bend. "I personally do not believe in wildlife management—wildlife manage themselves. We can only manage humans. We can only communicate with humans, by telling them what they should do to provide a healthy environment for wildlife."

Mohamad Azlan has never actually seen a wild tiger, but he's come plenty close, thank you very much.

"It was about six in the evening and I really had to check one of the cameras that had been overdue for two days," he says. "As I was squatting to check the number of shots taken, I suddenly heard a loud roar about 10 meters away. If the tiger wanted to attack me it could have done so easily — it just wanted to warn me off. That's good enough for me."

Azlan knows he doesn't need to make visual contact in order to study tigers. "I spend most of my day in the forest identifying possible sites to deploy infrared cameras to photograph tigers and prey. In the evening, I visit the farmers to talk about the problems they are facing. I also provide information about tiger movements and advise them not to allow their livestock to roam near tiger-prone areas.

"I've always felt the presence of tigers in the forest," Azlan says. "And we see pugmarks almost every day, some only a few hours old. Sometimes you even smell their presence."

Azlan's work is difficult, but he soldiers on because he understands how much it matters. "I have been interested in wildlife since I was young, but I never imagined that I would be working to save a species. I really feel someone has to do something before it's too late."

MAN-EATERS

Tigers generally avoid people and don't normally have a taste for their flesh, but they do occasionally kill and eat humans.

There are a couple of reasons tigers become man-eaters. People may unwittingly get between a mother and her young, and a female will attack anything that appears to threaten her cubs. Tigers that are wounded (often by bullets), old, ill or otherwise unable to catch swifter animals may also attack humans.

In many range states, tigers are so rare and so unlikely to encounter humans that they pose virtually no threat. That's not the case in India, though. And in the Sundarbans, a mangrove forest region of India and Bangladesh, they kill 50 or more people every year. For some reason, this population of tigers is particularly aggressive towards humans.

People who go into the Sundarbans to collect wood, honey or fish have come up with some techniques to discourage attacks. In the 1980s, some wore face masks on the backs of their heads in order to confuse the tiger, which usually attacks from behind. To train the animals to avoid people, villagers have set up human-shaped dummies attached to batteries that give a tiger a painful shock if it attacks. In other areas, electrified fences keep the predators away.

Since encounters between tigers and humans can result in harm coming to one or both, learning to minimize contact is an important step in tiger conservation.

∧ Accused of killing five people, this tiger rubbed its face raw on the bars of its cage after being captured in Sumatra in 2002.

< In the Sundarbans, wearing masks has not always prevented people from being killed by tigers, which for unknown reasons are particularly deadly to humans in that region.

47

Early in the last century, three tiger subspecies inhabited the islands of Indonesia. With the Bali and Javan tigers now extinct, only one remains. But if history isn't on the side of *Panthera tigris sumatrae*, at least Ronald Tilson is.

Tilson, Director of Conservation at the Minnesota Zoo, is the originator of the Sumatran Tiger Conservation Program, an international effort supporting Indonesia's attempt to save the last of the island subspecies. In the early 1990s, the best estimate of the Sumatran tiger's numbers was 500 to 600 animals. Then, in 1997, the Indonesian economy collapsed, leaving people desperately trying to earn a living.

> "The farmers understand the issues. But when your children are starving you will do what is necessary."

"Because of extensive poaching since then, tiger numbers have decreased considerably," Tilson says. Most of the problems occur just outside the national parks, where there is no enforcement of the laws designed to protect wildlife. "Villagers are going in and trapping the prey, starting small gardens and cutting wood. And it's here where you have all the tiger-people conflict. Once tigers start killing the cattle or goats or dogs, the local villagers put out poison. Half of the tigers in the local black market have probably come from this source."

While conservation projects in other countries have made a priority of raising awareness, Tilson says that the time for this has passed in Sumatra. "Under these conditions, education and outreach is impossible." Besides, the problem isn't ignorance, it's poverty. "The farmers understand the issues. But when your children are starving you will do what is necessary—including illegal things—to feed them."

The program uses remote cameras to monitor the island's tigers and their prey, so it can help protect remaining habitat. It has also trained patrols to discourage poaching, but killings are still rampant.

In August 2002, Tilson and other conservationists publicly set fire to stuffed Sumatran tigers and other confiscated specimens to protest the weak enforcement of wildlife protection laws. Though the problem hasn't gone away, their action did have some effect. Within six months of the bonfire, two poachers were fined and jailed — something once almost unheard of in Indonesia.

A lot depends on the country's economy, which is beyond the control of conservation groups. In any case, Tilson, who has worked in Indonesia since 1964, feels that long-term plans must be managed locally, not by scientists from across the ocean. "I have a very good relationship with my Indonesian colleagues, but eventually I would like to step away and leave it all to the Indonesians."

∧ Ron Tilson (*right*) is one of the key tiger-conservation figures in Indonesia, where he has done fieldwork for almost 40 years.

In the world of tiger conservation, you might say that Sarah Christie has earned her stripes.

Christie manages conservation projects for the Zoological Society of London, for over a decade she's headed up the Amur and Sumatran tiger breeding and programs in Europe and Australasia. She also oversees field projects in Sumatra and Russia for 21st Century Tiger, a British conservation group. "I have a history of biting off far too much," she says wryly.

Originally trained as a zookeeper, Christie is one of the world's top experts in managing captive tiger populations. Part of her role is simply making sure cubs have a good home. "I have to recommend every year that the majority of zoos do not breed, because we wouldn't know where to put all the cubs."

More importantly, she is a matchmaker for captive tigers. All mammals benefit from genetic diversity—in other words, they're less healthy when mating occurs between close relatives. This is called inbreeding, and it tends to make animals less fertile and more vulnerable to disease and defects. "For zoos to fulfill their conservation functions, you need to have a population that remains viable in the long term."

Christie also believes that tigers from different subspecies should not breed together. To ensure this, she keeps a studbook on about 220 Amur tigers in 21 countries, and 115 Sumatran tigers in 13 countries. "Each animal has a number and a record, which includes the numbers of its parents," she explains. When she can trace the family tree back to a wild ancestor, that animal is called a founder. The more founder genes present, the healthier the captive population.

Many captive tigers are hybrids of more than one subspecies, and some suffer from inbreeding. Programs like those run by Sarah Christie ensure the genetic diversity of zoo tigers.

Christie has worked hard to unite conservationists in Asia, Europe and North America. In 1998, she began compiling a database of tiger projects that has since become global. "I ended up traveling halfway around the world, visiting the range states to get details. It took a couple of years, but I did do it."

Today, several governments and conservation groups use the database in their planning, and there's talk of expanding it to include other cat species. Is Christie going to take that on, too? "You've got to be kidding," she says, smiling. "Even I wouldn't go that far."

TIGERS IN CAPTIVITY

Everyone involved in saving the tiger agrees that the most critical work is being done in the forests of Asia. However, zoos can play an important role as well.

Thousands of tigers live in zoos throughout the world—the captive populations of Amur and South China tigers, in fact, exceed those in the wild. Almost all were born in captivity, and those caught in the wild were rescue missions: animals confiscated from poachers, orphaned cubs, or tigers that have killed people or livestock and would otherwise have been shot. Still, some argue that the resources spent on captive animals would be better spent in the wild.

But that argument implies that zoos and field projects are in competition, says Sarah Christie. "The captive population I manage produces conservation support for wild tigers, rather than diverting resources from it. I think we can honestly say we're adding to the pool of money available, rather than taking from it."

In addition to raising funds, zoos play a critical role in educating the public. "It's the only place the vast majority of humans are ever going to see a tiger," Christie says. That's true not only in the West, but in tiger-range countries, too. "I've seen people in southeast Asia who have been unaware, until they've gone to the local zoo, that there were tigers in their country."

Zoologists who study captive tigers' behavior and biology also use that knowledge to contribute to conservation projects. For example, zoo scientists developed the anesthetic that allows field researchers to fit tigers with radio collars.

WHITE AND WRONG?

In 1951, the Maharaja of Rewa, an Indian prince, captured
a tiger cub with a remarkable appearance: it was creamy
white, with dark brown stripes, blue eyes and a pink nose.
It was not an albino; it was an extremely rare color variation
of the Indian tiger, born of two parents that carried a
mutant recessive gene.

The maharaja named the cub Mohan and quickly learned
how to breed more white tigers. The unique animal's first visit
to an American zoo in 1960 was an instant hit, and today
zoos and circuses around the world exhibit white tigers.

While these animals have their own rare beauty, many
conservationists object to breeding white tigers in captivity.
It is an unnatural process, they argue, having more to do
with creating a spectacle for profit than with trying to save
an endangered species.

Finally—though everyone hopes this will never be necessary—a well-managed
captive population is a genetic lifeboat, in case the wild population ever disappears.
"It would be utterly irresponsible of the world's zoos to fail to maintain that
reservoir of genetic material," Christie says. "I think we need every tool in the
conservation toolbox to save tigers or other endangered species, and this is one."

BACK TO THE WILD?

While wild tigers face enormous obstacles, the animal itself is in little danger of absolute extinction. That's because tigers breed extremely well in captivity. But can captive-born tigers ever be released into the wild?

^ By 2008, the Chinese will attempt to introduce captive-born tigers to the wild, a difficult and controversial plan.

Similar schemes have shown promising results. Wolves and cougars have been reintroduced successfully, and the Chinese are planning to try it with tigers by 2008. Still, the idea continues to be controversial. "Reintroduction of large carnivores is difficult, expensive and time-consuming," Sarah Christie says. "And while it's not impossible for tigers, we're certainly doing everything we can to avoid getting to that point."

To begin with, the problem facing tigers is not too few wild animals, it's too little habitat and too little prey. In areas that are truly protected from human activities like hunting, farming and logging, tiger populations can and do recover on their own. Introducing tigers into areas where these activities continue would solve nothing in the long term.

The other chief worry is that captive tigers are too familiar with people. Without their natural fear of humans, they may pose a real threat to villagers and their livestock. And when people see tigers as a threat, they respond with traps and rifles. "Any big cat that is not afraid of people is a *dead* big cat," Christie says.

Christie, Ron Tilson and others have suggested ways to overcome these hurdles. Cubs could be raised with virtually no human contact—in large enclosures stocked with prey, where they would learn to hunt as they grew up. It would be at least one generation before these animals could safely be moved into the wild.

Tigers might be conditioned to avoid livestock; researchers have experimented with electric shocks and illness-causing additives for domestic animal meat. Perhaps specially designed radio collars could confine them to territory uninhabited by people.

Nobody knows whether these methods will work, but they offer some hope that, given the right conditions, dwindling wild populations could someday be given a boost.

WHAT IS THE TIGER'S FUTURE?

Many people thought the wild tiger would be extinct by the new millennium. And it likely would have been if not for the intervention of conservationists, many of whom have put their lives in jeopardy to stop the trade in tiger parts. These scientists, rangers and government officers have demonstrated—particularly in India and Russia—that a well-managed conservation plan can revive populations.

"Tigers are not yet a lost cause, by any means."

"All the doomsday prophecies about the tiger's extinction in the past 70 years have been proven wrong," says Ullas Karanth in India. "Tigers are not yet a lost cause, by any means."

But complacency is as much an enemy as guns and chainsaws. Ensuring a future for the tiger doesn't mean throwing people and money at the problem, and then leaving as soon as there are positive results. It means protecting habitat, keeping a constant eye on wild populations and being sensitive to the people who live alongside tigers. There are solutions, but none fits every situation. "We cannot build a model that forecasts the future of tigers," Karanth insists, "because human will, chance and the ecological resilience of tigers all play such a major role."

Many tiger-range countries are overpopulated and terribly poor, and improving the economy isn't something that well-intentioned nature lovers can do. But hunting and habitat destruction are human activities, and they are within our control.

Because of the work done so far, the king of the cats will be around to see the next Year of the Tiger in 2010. And with dedication and international cooperation, it can survive into the next millennium and beyond. If humans have pushed the wild tiger to the brink, humans can pull it back.

FAST FACTS

Scientific name •	*Panthera tigris* (abbreviated *Pt* in subspecies names below)
Subspecies •	from largest to smallest: Amur or Siberian (*Pt altaica*); Indian or Bengal (*Pt tigris*); Indochinese (*Pt corbetti*); South China or Chinese (*Pt amoyensis*); Sumatran (*Pt sumatrae*)
Size •	length, including tail, ranges from 7 feet (2 m) in small females to more than 10 feet (3 m) in large males
•	weight ranges from 165 pounds (75 kg) in small females to 660 pounds (300 kg) in large males
Life span •	about 15 years in the wild; 20 years in captivity
Locomotion •	too heavy to run at full speed for long distances, but can sprint at 35 mph (55 kph) for several seconds
•	able to leap 30 feet (9 m) over level ground
Senses •	night vision about six times more sensitive than a human's
•	does not see colors well, but can sense very slight movements at eye level
•	excellent binocular vision: uses both eyes in tandem to estimate distance
•	sense of smell not well developed; plays only a minor role in hunting
•	can hear an enormous range of frequencies, from the ultrasonic calls of rodents (undetectable by humans) to the lower-pitched rustlings of an animal traveling through the brush
•	large ear flaps, called pinnae, help pinpoint the location of prey
•	whiskers around mouth, above eyes and on sides of face help in navigating in the dark and detecting the most vulnerable part of its prey's neck

Paws	• padded to allow for soft, silent steps
	• five digits on each forepaw, four on each hind foot
	• retractable claws, used to take down prey and make territorial scratch marks
Teeth	• 16 on top and 14 on bottom in adults, set in a jaw that can only move up and down, not side to side
	• largest canine teeth of any predator: up to 3 inches (7.5 cm) long
	• incisors used to hold prey and tear meat from bone
	• premolars and molars used for crushing bone and chewing meat
	• two pairs of carnassial teeth, which work like scissors to slice meat
Reproduction	• mates at any time of year, but most often between November and April
	• gestation lasts about 100 days
	• litter size can range from one to seven cubs, but is typically two or three
	• cubs are born blind and weigh just 2 to 3 pounds (1 to 1.5 kg)

59

HOW YOU CAN HELP

If you would like to learn more about tigers or the projects designed to protect them, contact one the following organizations:

Hornocker Wildlife Institute
www.hwi.org

2023 Stadium Drive, Suite 1A, Bozeman, MT, U.S.A. 59715
Phone (888) TIGER44
Offers a Siberian tiger adoption kit for $26.95 (U.S.), which includes a poster, a sticker, an educational brochure and a subscription to the quarterly *Tiger Tracks* newsletter.

Save China's Tigers
www.savechinastigers.org

P.O. Box 837, Berea, KY, U.S.A. 40403
Phone (866) 985-8887
The only charity devoted exclusively to the Chinese tiger, the rarest of all the subspecies. Also has an office in the U.K.

The Tiger Foundation
www.tigers.ca

1177 West Hastings Street, Suite 2007, Vancouver, BC, Canada v6E 2K3
Phone (604) 893-8718
Inspired by a child's wish to stop the tiger trade, this organization promotes conservation education and helps to fund projects in Sumatra and elsewhere.

Tiger Information Center
www.5tigers.org

Phone (888) 5-TIGERS
The most comprehensive Web site about tigers, including up-to-date research news and special sections for kids and teachers.

21st Century Tiger
www.21stcenturytiger.org

c/o Zoological Society of London
Regents Park, London NW1 4RY, United Kingdom
Phone +44 20 7449 6444
Supports conservation projects in several tiger-range states, including Sumatra, India, Russia, Cambodia and Malaysia.

WildAid
www.wildaid.org

450 Pacific Avenue, Suite 201, San Francisco, CA, U.S.A. 94133
Phone (415) 834-3174
An international organization whose Vladivostok chapter helped organize Russia's Inspection Tiger project. Sends a free electronic newsletter on request.

World Wildlife Fund US
www.worldwildlife.org

1250 Twenty-Fourth Street NW, P.O. Box 97180, Washington, DC, U.S.A. 20090-7180
Phone (888) CALL-WWF
Features on-line fact sheets about pandas and other endangered species, electronic postcards, and a free Action Kit offer (U.S. only).

World Wildlife Fund Canada
www.wwfcanada.org

245 Eglinton Avenue East, Suite 410, Toronto, ON, Canada M4P 3J1
Phone (888) 26-PANDA or (416) 489-8800
Offers on-line tips on getting involved in conservation efforts, as well as classroom activities. WWF Canada is also headquarters for the North American chapter of TRAFFIC, which monitors the illicit trade in tigers and other wildlife.

Wildlife Conservation Society
wcs.org

2300 Southern Boulevard, Bronx, NY, U.S.A. 10460
Phone (718) 220-5100
The WCS has been involved in many tiger projects since helping sponsor George Schaller's pioneering study the 1960s.

INDEX

PHOTO CREDITS

AUTHOR'S NOTE

This book is dedicated with love to my son Erick.

Writing this book has given me the privilege of working with dedicated and generous people in India, Malaysia, the United Kingdom and Russia as well as the United States and Canada. I am particularly grateful to Sarah Christie, Ullas Karanth and Ron Tilson — all among the top tiger conservationists in the world — for sharing their time and expertise.

Thanks also to Mohamad Azlan, Sergei Bereznuk, Praveen Bhargav, Steve Brearton, Cao Dan, Nathalie Chalifour, Tatiana Dmitrenko, Sarah Emery, Judy Mills, Li Quan, Melanie Shepherd and Janet Tilson.